Color

by Kay Manolis

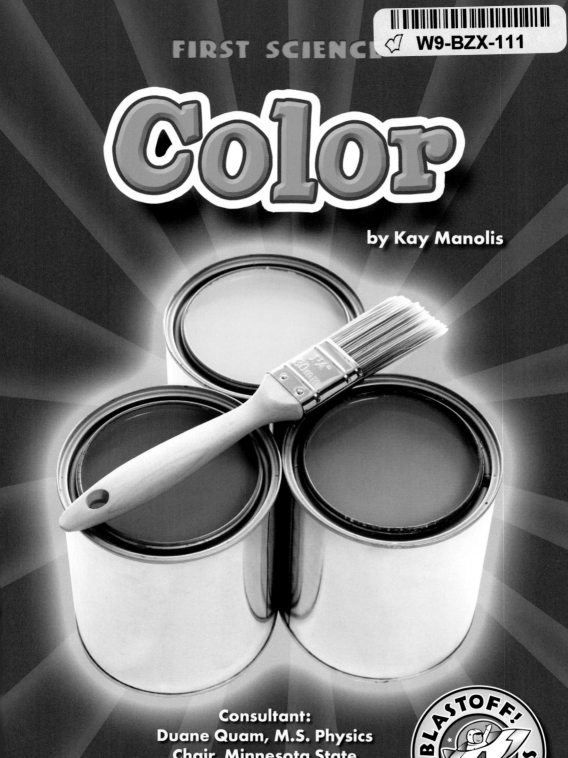

Consultant:
Duane Quam, M.S. Physics
Chair, Minnesota State
Academic Science Standards
Writing Committee

BLASTOFF! READERS
4

BELLWETHER MEDIA • MINNEAPOLIS, MN

Note to Librarians, Teachers, and Parents:

Blastoff! Readers are carefully developed by literacy experts and combine standards-based content with developmentally appropriate text.

Level 1 provides the most support through repetition of high-frequency words, light text, predictable sentence patterns, and strong visual support.

Level 2 offers early readers a bit more challenge through varied simple sentences, increased text load, and less repetition of high-frequency words.

Level 3 advances early-fluent readers toward fluency through increased text and concept load, less reliance on visuals, longer sentences, and more literary language.

Level 4 builds reading stamina by providing more text per page, increased use of punctuation, greater variation in sentence patterns, and increasingly challenging vocabulary.

Level 5 encourages children to move from "learning to read" to "reading to learn" by providing even more text, varied writing styles, and less familiar topics.

Whichever book is right for your reader, Blastoff! Readers are the perfect books to build confidence and encourage a love of reading that will last a lifetime!

This edition first published in 2016 by Bellwether Media, Inc.

No part of this publication may be reproduced in whole or in part without written permission of the publisher. For information regarding permission, write to Bellwether Media, Inc., Attention: Permissions Department, 6012 Blue Circle Dr., Minnetonka, MN 55343.

Library of Congress Cataloging-in-Publication Data
Manolis, Kay.
   Color / by Kay Manolis.
      p. cm. – (Blastoff! readers: First science)
   Includes bibliographical references and index.
   Summary: "Simple text and full-color photographs introduce beginning readers to color. Developed by literacy experts for students in kindergarten through third grade"–Provided by publisher.
   ISBN: 978-1-60014-227-7 (hardcover : alk. paper)
   ISBN: 978-0-531-28450-6 (paperback : alk. paper)
   1. Color–Juvenile literature. I. Title.

QC495.5.M365 2009
535.6–dc22   2008021301

Contents

What Is Color?

Look at all the colors in the world! Colors make the world more beautiful and interesting. The colors that you see are caused by light.

Light is all around you much of the time. Light comes from **sources** such as light bulbs or the sun. Light travels in straight lines through the air. It travels in every direction away from sources.

Sunlight and most electric lights are called **white lights** because they do not appear to have any color. They are actually made up of many colors that you normally cannot see. These colors are called the **spectrum**. The spectrum is made of these six colors: red, orange, yellow, green, blue, and violet.

The colors in the spectrum can be seen when a stream of light bends a little. A **prism** is a glass tool that bends light and separates it into all its colors.

! **fun fact**

Sir Isaac Newton was a scientist who lived in the 1600s. He was the first to show that white light is made up of many colors. He used a prism to separate sunlight into its many colors.

Light allows you to see the world. When light hits objects, some of it **reflects**, or bounces off. Some reflected light enters your eyes. Then you see the objects.

Reflected light is also what allows you to see colors. Every object reflects some of the colors of light and **absorbs**, or soaks in, other colors. For example, a red object reflects mostly red light. It absorbs the other colors. So only red light reaches your eyes.

This balloon reflects the color yellow and absorbs other colors. That is why you see yellow.

What colors do these flowers reflect?

! **fun fact**

Fireworks are made of chemicals that turn colors when they burn.

Leaves contain a green **chemical** in the summer. This chemical helps plants make food from sunlight, air, and water. It also reflects green light. You see a lot of green in nature!

In the fall, plants don't make the green chemicals. Then you see other colors that were hidden by the green. Leaves may reflect red, orange, and yellow light now.

Some things reflect all the colors of light equally. You see those things as pure white.

Some things absorb all the colors of light. You see those things as pure black.

Animals and Color

Colors help some animals stay safe. Many wild animals have a color that matches the color of their surroundings. This helps them hide from other animals that may want to eat them.

Animals may use color to give information. Bright colors such as red and orange warn other animals of danger. For example, an animal would get very sick if it ate this poison dart frog. The frog's bright colors warn other animals not to eat it!

Colors Are Helpful

People use colors to give information. When you see a red street light or stop sign, you know to stop. Green means go.

Orange warning signs attract peoples' attention. This is important in places where people need to be careful.

Colors can also express feelings. What kinds of feelings do you think the artist was expressing in this painting?

How do you use colors?

Glossary

absorb—to take in or soak up

chemical—a substance that can cause a change in another substance

prism—a glass tool that bends light and separates it into many colors; a prism can also cause separated colors to mix together again into light.

reflect—to bounce off; when light hits an object, it reflects back in another direction.

sources—things that give off light; the main source of light on Earth is the sun.

spectrum—the range of colors that make up white light

white light—light that is made up of all colors but appears to have no color

To Learn More

AT THE LIBRARY
Helman, Andrea. *Wild Colors.* Seattle, Wash.: Sasquatch Books, 2003.

Jenkins, Steve. *Living Color.* New York: Houghton Mifflin, 2007.

Riley, Peter. *Light and Color.* New York: Franklin Watts, 2006.

ON THE WEB
Learning more about color is as easy as 1, 2, 3.

1. Go to www.factsurfer.com

2. Enter "color" into search box.

3. Click the "Surf" button and you will see a list of related web sites.

With factsurfer.com, finding more information is just a click away.

Index

The images in this book are reproduced through the courtesy of: Juan Martinez, front cover, pp. 12, 14, 15, 19, 20-21; Racheal Grazias, pp. 4-5; Chris Rogers - Rainbow / Getty Images, pp. 6-7; Age fotostock, pp. 8-9; Guy Bubb / Getty Images, p. 10; Alan Levenson / Getty Images, p. 11; bornholm, p. 13; Gerry Ellis / Getty Images, p. 16; Kevin Scahfer / Alamy, p. 17; Jonathan Larsen, p. 18.